Growing up Friendly

STEVEN EUGENE WINTERS

authorHOUSE®

AuthorHouse™
1663 Liberty Drive
Bloomington, IN 47403
www.authorhouse.com
Phone: 1 (800) 839-8640

Published by AuthorHouse 11/19/2019

ISBN: 978-1-7283-3682-4 (sc)
ISBN: 978-1-7283-3680-0 (hc)
ISBN: 978-1-7283-3681-7 (e)

Print information available on the last page.

This book is printed on acid-free paper.

Contents

Welcome!

Sitting quietly at the southern end of Tyler County is the tiny town of Friendly, West Virginia. Nestled between the rolling hills to the east and the Ohio River to the west, her inhabitants exhibit a unique blend of old Appalachia and modern living. Although technology exists here, the town still has the same look and feel as it did when I lived there fifty years ago. There are still gardens and livestock within the city limits, and people know each other on a first-name basis. While it is not a town caught up in its past, it is a town that insists on preserving a part of it.

The fact that you are reading this book gives me great pleasure. I am humbled and thankful. But be forewarned, I do not have a degree in journalism. I am simply a man who enjoys telling stories. This likely will not be a *New York Times* Best Seller. I am a self-taught writer, and I am a man of few words. While a professional writer will lure you into their story with fancy words that come from a thesaurus, I prefer to keep mine simple. I don't reckon you need three pages of fluff and fill to tell you how the inside of a room looks. In other "words" (get it?), I will tell you my story and allow you to fill in the background using your own imagination and memories.

Eloquent (graceful) prose is wonderful, and as an avid reader, I appreciate it. It's just not my forte (that means it's not my thing). I don't think you'll need fancy words to understand my story. In fact, I'm betting you won't. So from here on out, I won't use any words that might make you stop reading and reach for a dictionary.

As you read this book, you may experience similar connections to your own youth, and that's my goal. I want to take you back in time. I want you to remember. I believe it is important to exercise your mind and relive those wonderful, youthful memories through the fading lens of time. Hopefully, some of those memories will return in full focus. Please take those memories and share them with your family. Oral history is a vital yet rapidly fading part of our society. Everything we do today is shared online, and personal connections are becoming a thing of the past.

I will not attempt to prove that the "good old days" of my youth were better than today. The world is very different now, and in many ways, much better. Instead, I prefer to think of the days of my youth as simpler times.

Life was slower. Needs far outweighed wants. People connected on a much more personal level.

As you prepare to turn the page, I'll explain the title of this book. When I started playing baseball, the only Little League was in nearby Sistersville. During our first game, I overheard one parent asking another, "Who is that boy playing first base?" The other parent replied, "Oh, he's a Friendly boy."

Indeed I was. This is my story about growing up there, in Friendly, over the period from 1968 to 1972. I focus on this particular time period because some of my most vivid memories of my youth occurred at this time. Both good and bad, they remain strong within my heart to this day. The stories are not written in the exact order in which they occurred. After all, it has been fifty years, so please bear with me. Hopefully you will find yourself smiling and laughing at my adventures. They are all true, and they are written with love. I hope you enjoy!

The Hail Mary

A One-In-A-Million Throw

It was a hot and humid day. Summer was in full swing, and my brother Mark and I were arguing over some stupid topic as we stood near the edge of WV State Route 2, the two-lane main artery which ran through our town. Mark was fifteen months older than me, and he took his looks from our dad. I favored mom, so it was no surprise that Mark and I quarreled often, as we were as different in temperament as we were in looks. Although I was smaller in stature, I was faster, and I had inherited the stubbornness of the Winters' family genes. The competitive edge closed between us as I grew older, and Mark became more resentful toward me.

On this particular day, he was accompanied by his friend. As the argument escalated, I quickly realized that I was outnumbered, and so I decided that flight was the best option. As I began to run away, Mark and his friend began to pelt me with rocks, a few of which bounced off my back and legs—but I was in high gear, and I knew I could outrun them.

Our house was about one hundred yards away, and I summoned all the energy my young legs could generate. As I raced down that dirt road, I could hear the rocks landing just behind me. Encouraged by this, and nearing our front yard, I let up just a bit…and that's when I felt the pain.

Mark had unleashed one final throw, and that rock traveled true, straight, and far, striking me on the top of my head. How he'd managed to throw a rock so far and so accurately astounds me to this day, but he did. I ran to the back door of our house, then entered the kitchen. Mom was on the phone, but when she turned toward me, she dropped the receiver on the floor. Her face turned ashen, and then she screamed, "What happened?"

"Mark hit me on the head with a rock," I sobbed.

I was actually feeling very little pain, mind you. But we all know that any cuts to the head produce a lot of blood, and apparently there were great amounts of it flowing down my face. When Mark came home, there was hell to pay. I stood outside his bedroom door later that day when dad came home from work to administer the punishment which my brother so richly deserved...a whipping with a belt. As my dad rained down blow after blow, a smile spread across my face. It was a light bulb appearing over the head moment. If I could not best my bigger and stronger brother in battle, I could always rat him out to mom. She was the great equalizer, and this sibling rivalry had just taken a turn in my favor. I will have more to say about my older sibling later.

Christmas Day

My Highs and Lows

❧•••❧

When you're an elementary school student, the excitement of Christmas begins to build as soon as school lets out for the holidays. The next two weeks are magical. It's the anticipation that really grabs you, though. Mom always got the entire family involved with decorating the tree. My job was draping the long, metallic-silver icicles over the outside of the tree after the ornaments and lights had been placed. Of course, the tree was always real. There was no place in my mom's world for fake Christmas trees. The scent of pine filled the house, and in my mind, once the tree was up, it was game on!

Mom would ask each of us what we wanted for Christmas. This was considered to be the most important decision my siblings and I would make all year, because back then, we only got one special gift from Santa. When I say only one, you must trust me. There would be multiple wrapped gifts under the tree on Christmas morning, but the ones from Santa were left unwrapped. We knew that the wrapped gifts were often clothes, and we had no interest in them. But that one special gift was what we dreamed about. Careful thought and consideration went into our decisions.

The year I turned nine, I wished for a Lite Brite (Most of you may remember this, but you youngsters can Google it). To my delight, it was waiting for me under the tree when I came downstairs on Christmas morning. Although many of the multicolored pegs would eventually find their way into mom's vacuum cleaner over the coming months, I truly enjoyed it.

The following Christmas neared and I wished for a Hot Wheels race set, with two cars and a looping track. That was also the year my brother informed me that Santa Claus was not real. Well, I kind of suspected that already, but he insisted on proving it to me. In my bedroom there was a door that led to the attic. Mark led me up the dark steps and pointed to a large cardboard box. "Go ahead, look inside," he said. I did, and there before my eyes was a brand new Hot Wheels set.

"See? Dad buys the presents and mom hides them up here. Then on Christmas Eve, after we go to bed, she brings them downstairs and puts them under the tree."

I was mildly upset as I faced the fact that Santa was not real, but I was thrilled that I would be getting the present I wanted the most. I was into cars, and that present brought many, many hours of enjoyment.

The following Christmas, dad placed a lock on the attic door. I don't know how he figured it out, but it was clear we weren't going to spoil any surprises this time. This was also the year that mom declared there would be no going downstairs before sunrise to view our presents.

This was disturbing, because Mark and I had mastered the art of sneaking down the three flights of stairs on Christmas morning without making a sound. We practiced over and over, placing little slips of paper on each step that creaked or groaned. We would memorize each spot, and eventually we mastered the silent descent.

Fully confident, we began our quest. It was 4:30 a.m., and we had not slept a wink. We stole quietly to the top of the stairs, gave each other a nod, then took the first step. Mom's voice rang out loudly from her bedroom, "You boys get your butts back in bed. Now!"

Crestfallen, we slinked back to our rooms. I remember waiting for dawn to break, which seemed like an eternity. Finally, the first rays of sunlight appeared, and I leapt from my bed. Mark was already waiting for me at the top of the stairs. We didn't try to disguise our steps this time, as we bounded down to the living room.

But the wait had been worth it. There, under the twinkling lights of the tree, was the one present I had hoped for, but dared not expect. It was a Demolition Derby race set. Basically, it was a figure-eight race track with two battery-powered cars. The cars would race around until they would inevitably meet in the middle and crash. The cars had molded plastic fenders which would fly off on impact, but you could easily snap them back on and begin racing again.

It was the best Christmas present I had ever received. As I opened the box and began assembling the track, I realized that I had no batteries. Once the track was complete, I resigned myself to waiting. It was frustrating, but I was so excited that it didn't matter. As I visualized the cars flying around the track, Mark jumped up and stepped over me. In doing so, he stepped on, and crushed, both my plastic cars. The ultimate Christmas present was ruined.

The next year, I did not wish for anything. I told my mom that anything would be fine. On Christmas Eve, it snowed. I remember looking out my bedroom window and marveling at the deepening white blanket covering everything I could see. I had no expectations that Christmas, but the snow was, in itself, a special present. The moonlight reflecting off the surface of that snowy cover made the night look like early evening. They say that Christmas snow is magical, and I still believe that to this day.

My present that Christmas was a record player. Mom had included two 45-rpm records. One was "The Little

Drummer Boy," and the other was by a group called "Chicago." I've never figured out why she selected those two records, but I played them over and over in my room.

Another upside to Christmas, of course, was our grandparents. After the day had passed, there were the obligatory visits from family. As kids, we viewed these visits with mixed emotions. We knew there would be many wrapped gifts, and those were never good. Wrapped gifts from your grandparents were usually socks, underwear, jeans, etc. Granted, it was a gift, but even a child can figure out that these gifts were simply a wish list from your parents to *their* parents.

Still, spending time with our grandparents was special, and both of my Mamaws always brought baked goodies with them. To this day, my Mamaw Christopher still sends homemade cookies and candy to me by mail. It is always my favorite Christmas gift, because it's made with love.

You can take whatever memories you want from your past and place them in whatever order you like. Christmas has been, and always will be, my favorite holiday. That special toy that was broken should have been my worst memory, and yet it is my favorite. I got the present I had wished for, and that's all we can really hope for.

What we do with our memories is up to us.

Friendly Elementary

A.K.A. Friendly Tech

❊

Standing two stories high and featuring white slate siding, two separate front entrances, and a bell tower, the town school was already well aged when I attended my first class. When you entered, two distinct odors immediately caught your attention: the smell of oiled wooden floors, and rotten eggs. That rotten egg smell was from the well water the school used. It permeated throughout the building, especially near the restrooms. The lone water fountains on each floor went mainly unused, their porcelain bowls stained dark yellow from the water. I tried one once, and never sipped another drop.

There were two classrooms on the top floor for the older kids, which could be accessed by a rickety stairway that groaned with every step. The first floor included a classroom for the younger kids, and a lunchroom. The playground area outside had swings, monkey bars, and ample space to play. There was a small, separate gym, built from cement blocks, which included a basketball court (The gym stands to this day. The school was not so lucky, as it's been torn down).

So the immediate problem for me was, if I can't drink the water, how will I survive? Enter the lunch ladies. Every morning, around 10:00 a.m., they would bring milk to our classroom. This was known as a milk break, during which we would select a pint of white or chocolate milk, packaged in those little cardboard containers, from the rolling cart and do nothing for the next fifteen minutes except drink our milk quietly. For this luxury, we paid five cents a day. I was confused at first, because when one of the lunch ladies asked me if I wanted white or chocolate, I thought it was a trick. Of course I wanted chocolate! There were always a few kids who didn't have the money for these milk breaks, but the teachers would always pay for them out of their own pockets.

While I'm talking about the lunch ladies, let me tell you this: There were never two nicer ladies to grace the halls of Friendly Tech. During lunch, we would grab a tray and go through a serving line. After we all sat down and began eating, these ladies would circulate among us, replacing bread and milk and whatever else we had finished. They made sure our bellies were full, and no kid ever went hungry. My favorite lunch was potato soup. They would serve it with a side of peanut butter sandwiches and wedges of cheddar cheese. I often ate two bowls, and to this day I eat a peanut butter sandwich with my potato soup.

While many of the memories from my four years there have faded, the lunch ladies and several more memories remain clear, like the time my friend Mike Davis was supposed to be studying in fifth-grade Study Hall. The teacher, Perry Leach, was walking quietly around the room, peering over our shoulders to see what we were reading. Mike was not reading anything. He was drawing a cartoon. Mr. Leach stopped behind him, but Mike was oblivious to his presence. Mr. Leach reached down and snatched the drawing from Mike's desk. He held it up and asked, "What is this supposed to be?" Mike replied, "It's a monster. A freak." Mr. Leach smiled and said, "Well, it is a good drawing, but freak is spelled F.R.E.A.K. You spelled it F.R.E.K." And thus Mike Davis' nickname was born. From that moment, until he graduated high school, he was known as "Freck."

Another lasting memory happened during my sixth-grade year. I had tried out for the basketball team, and I'd been selected. Of course, only six boys tried out, so in retrospect, it wasn't a big deal. By this point in my life, I was a big sports fan, but basketball was not my specialty. Oh sure, I knew how to play it, but I lacked the basic skills...like dribbling and running at the same time. We were playing a game against Sistersville, and they were heavy favorites. They had sharp-looking orange and black uniforms, and twelve team members. We had ragtag green uniforms with the team name, "Trojans," written across the front in stitched lettering that threatened to fall off at any moment. Somehow, we beat them. I think it was probably the worst basketball game ever played. The final score was something like 15 to 12. But I did score on a free throw in that game, which also happened to be the one and only point I scored in my Trojans career.

One of the perks of being a sixth-grader at Friendly Tech was the ringing of the school bell. We were assigned this task on a rotating basis, and there was no greater job. When you walked up those old stairs to the second floor, there was a rope that dangled down from the bell tower and was hooked to the wall near the top. Upon a cue from the principal, you would take hold of the rope and give it two hard yanks. This was done first thing in the morning to announce the start of the school day, then again twice at midday to signal the start and end of lunch, and finally one last time to announce the dismissal of classes in the afternoon. It gave us a sense of importance and responsibility.

Friendly Tech shaped me in many ways. I learned that teachers and staff always had the best interests of the students in mind. I witnessed caring and dedicated adults on a daily basis. When you're exposed to that at a young age, it sticks with you. Education isn't always about learning from books. Sometimes it's about imitating the behavior of people you respect. Kind acts are contagious. I learned that in elementary school.

The House

Arriving in Friendly

❖

We had lived in several homes before we wound up in Friendly. While they were all good-sized, nothing could prepare me for the castle which would become my favorite home. It was a well-built, two-story, wooden home, with five bedrooms and a bathroom upstairs. The downstairs included a front parlor, living room, den, kitchen, dining room, and another bathroom. There was a covered porch off of the living room, and another one off of the kitchen, which led to a small, detached building/shop. This small building was where mom did our laundry.

The fact that all four of us kids would have our own bedrooms was the best part of moving here. The only thing that concerned me about my new room was the old door which led up to the attic. On one of the first nights we stayed in our new home, there was a storm. I was awakened in the middle of the night by flashes of lightning and claps of thunder. I could hear the wind howling outside as the raindrops pelted against the windows. Then, the attic door moaned, creaked, and shook. I leapt from my bed and ran down the hall to my parents' bedroom.

Mom was already out of bed, as my sister Sara had arrived before me. Mom assured us that everything was okay. It was only a bad storm. I explained to mom that I wasn't worried about the storm. I was more concerned about the ghouls and goblins that were trying to open the attic door and kill me! After mom tucked Sara back into her bed, she led me back to my room. She switched on my bedroom light and walked over to the attic door. She turned and beckoned me to join her. I was shaking with fear, but mom had that calm smile on her face that told me it was okay.

She opened the attic door and started up into the darkness. I was amazed at her bravery. Halfway up the attic steps, she reached for a cord that hung from a single lightbulb. She gave it a yank, and the cavernous darkness of the rafters was lit up. I looked around, fully expecting a skeleton to come rushing toward us. Mom took my hand and led me to the top of the steps. "There, you see? There's nothing up here but us, and maybe a few mice. But a mouse can't hurt you."

Seeing the attic bathed in light, I relaxed. Mom explained that the wind made the attic door shake. She assured me that there was nothing to fear. When we returned to my room, mom whispered, "This is an old house, and sometimes it makes noises. But it will never harm you. This house will always protect you." I never feared the attic after that night, even though that old rickety door still woke me up now and then.

Mom seemed to have her finger on the pulse of that old farmhouse from the get-go. Despite the house only having a single natural gas floor furnace in the living room, she would arrange box fans all over to circulate heat throughout the house in the winter. In the summer, she was more creative, as we did not have air conditioning. She would go from room to room, opening and closing windows and blinds throughout the day. She had a system. The house was built before air conditioning was invented, so it was a simple method of closing the blinds and windows on the east side (sunrise) in the morning, and opening the windows on the west side. Then, as sunset neared, she would switch them around. By keeping the north- and south-facing windows open all the time, a breeze was created that lasted throughout the day.

I have many fond memories of that house, especially having a room to myself. I spent many hours reading and daydreaming in my room. There was one moment, as I lay there on my bed, that I can still recall to this day. I was pondering life, as only little boys can, when I made a promise to myself. I promised that, no matter what, I would always and forever remember that moment. I focused on it, and fifty years later, I can remember that moment clearly. I simply thought, "I will never forget this moment."

Clearly, that house was magical.

Card Parties

The Moms' Night Out

In the late 1960s, women were still mostly confined to the home, and men were the breadwinners. Mom didn't seem to mind her role as housekeeper. She was always busying herself with the laundry, with cleaning, and with cooking. Her only contact with the outside world was the rotary phone that hung on the kitchen wall. She had purchased an extra-long cord so that she could move about the kitchen and dining room freely, thus allowing her to multitask chores while catching up on the latest gossip with her friends.

When we first moved into the house, we were on a "party line," which meant the phone line was shared by others in the neighborhood. So if you wanted to make a call and picked up the receiver, you might hear someone talking. Most people were considerate and tried not to interrupt, but if it was important, they would ask you to please hang up for a few minutes so they could place their call. Of course, some people used the party line as a way to eavesdrop on their neighbors and gather gossip. Mom quickly tired of this and convinced dad to upgrade to a private line.

Soon after we moved to our house in Friendly, mom decided that my brother and I were capable of washing and drying the dinner dishes, so she assigned us those chores. I preferred to dry, as did my brother, but mom was wise enough to skirt that potential showdown by alternating us each week. She would occasionally ask us to run the sweeper as well, a task I did not mind. But for the most part, she did not involve us in the housework, except for that special day, once a month, when she would utter those terrible words: "The girls are coming over tonight to play cards."

Socializing back then meant getting together at someone's house, and playing cards was the entertainment. Now, I don't believe for a minute that there was any serious card-playing going on at that dining room table. But it was a big thing for mom, and in a way, it was her night out. After she uttered those dreaded words, we were put to work dusting, sweeping, and doing any other job mom could find for us. I never understood why it was so important for the house to be spotless. I mean, it was already clean!

The card game usually occurred on a Saturday night when the dads were all working the night shift at the plant. The exciting part for me was that each mom brought her kids with her, so my siblings and I had playmates for the evening. As the moms began arriving, the kids would be herded into the living room, where we had a television set. We would all sit on the floor and watch whatever show was on. You see, there was no such thing as cable back then, and we only received three channels. With luck, we would be able to watch a variety show, or maybe even a movie. To keep us quiet, mom would bring in a big bowl of potato chips and a can of French onion dip, and each of us would receive a glass of Pepsi. She would fill smaller bowls with chips from the bigger one, and give one to each kid.

Now, this was a big deal to us. We never got snacks at night, let alone soda pop! Just before the card game got into gear, mom would warn us to stay out of the dining room. We settled in and enjoyed our treats, with some kids eating quickly, and others eating slowly, savoring the experience. My brother ate his chips quickly, then sat back and studied the smaller kids in the room. Like a lion preparing to pounce on unsuspecting prey, he was selecting the weakest one in the herd. He slowly edged over to the youngest girl, who was intently watching the television. He snatched a handful of her chips in one lightning-fast grab, then retreated to his original spot.

As time passed, some of the other, younger kids fell asleep, and Mark moved in quickly to finish whatever chips they had left. While I watched him, it occurred to me that I was the only kid in the room who still had Pepsi left in my glass. I caught his eyes lingering on it, and I pulled the glass closer to me. But the lion was thirsty, and he moved with surprising quickness, grabbing my glass. He held it to his mouth, hesitated, then looked at me with an evil smile. Then, he licked the entire rim with his tongue and held it out to me. "Do you still want the rest of this?"

Enraged, my first thought was to hit him, but a fight between us would interrupt mom's card game, so I hatched another plan. I would simply go into the kitchen and get myself a new glass of Pepsi. But this required walking past the dining room, and six moms. The odds of sneaking past one mom were good, but six? I summoned what courage I could and slowly edged my way toward the kitchen. I peeked around the corner into the dining room, and what I saw confused me at first. There was so much cigarette smoke hanging in the air, it seemed as if the entire room was ablaze. If smoke detectors had been in use at that time, our home would have already been surrounded by fire trucks. The moms were talking and laughing loudly, and they seemed oblivious to my presence. So I darted into the kitchen and helped myself to a giant glass of Pepsi, plus some more chips from an open bag left on the counter.

I stood there and listened to the moms for a while. Their conversations were about their kids. I also suspected that whatever was in their glasses wasn't just Pepsi. I was glad I hadn't interrupted my mom's card game. They all needed each other, and they all needed a "night out" for themselves.

Roaming Free

Before Helicopter Moms

❧•❦

On a typical summer day in Friendly, I would wake up, make myself a bowl of cereal, then head outside. The day offered countless possibilities, and they were right there for the choosing. The beauty of childhood is not having an agenda. Sometimes I would play in the backyard with my Tonka trucks or little toy soldiers, using my imagination to create construction zones or battlefields.

But on my more adventurous days, I would climb the fence in our backyard and head into the hollow between the tall hills, following the small creek (It should be noted that "creek" was pronounced "crick" in Friendly). There were old logging trails which ran along the sides of the hills, and you could still make out the ruts made by wagons half a century before. I explored these trails, often finding artifacts left behind long ago. Most were just old bottles, but now and then I'd run across a special find, such as an old pair of eyeglasses, or a horseshoe.

Our family dog, a collie named Lady, would always accompany me on these treks. She never followed me, always staying ahead, as if she knew where I was headed. One particular day, I walked deeper than usual into the woods and spied an old cabin. It was not in good shape, and the roof had partially caved in. I became excited and began climbing the hillside toward it when Lady suddenly barked several times. I ignored her and kept climbing.

She walked toward me and barked again, but this time she also snapped at me, and I stopped in my tracks. Lady had never, ever made an aggressive move toward me. She turned away from me and began barking over and over. She seemed upset, and I was totally confused. Then I saw movement about ten feet in front of me: a six-foot-long copperhead snake was moving toward me.

Now, I was known to be a fast runner in those days, but when you're scared, fast shifts into a whole other gear. I was back down by the creek in seconds. I don't know if my feet actually touched the ground during my descent—I may have simply slid down the whole way! Lady stayed behind me as I splashed through the water, not daring to venture onto dry land for several hundred feet. When I finally stopped to catch my breath, Lady had taken up her usual spot ahead of me, so I knew I was safe. I never told mom this story, but I think she always knew something happened between me and Lady, because from that day forward, I always volunteered to feed and water my special gal.

When I wasn't exploring the woods, I enjoyed riding my bicycle. The highway was off limits, but when I asked mom if I could ride up Friendly Hill to visit my friend Mike Davis (Freck), she had no quarrel. As amazing as it may sound to some of you, the only rule she placed on me was to call her when I got there, and to call her when I was heading home. Now, Friendly Hill was a steep, winding monster. I had to push my bike to the top, because there was no way I could pedal up that imposing grade. There was a horseshoe bend near the bottom, and another just before the top. I didn't mind the walk up, because the ride back down would always be fast and exciting.

Freck and I would ride our bikes out toward Hissams Cabins, a few miles from his house. We would often ride for hours, exploring all of the side roads, not stopping until our stomachs told us it was time to eat. There was never a fear of strangers or abduction. The few cars we encountered on the road would give way to us, often with a beep of the horn and a wave from the driver. Even if we didn't know who they were, they all knew who we were. Friendly was a small place. After a nice supper at Freck's, I called my mom and let her know I was coming home.

As I pedaled the mile or so from Freck's house to the top of Friendly Hill, I felt a rush of adrenaline as I began to glide down. After easing slowly past the first horseshoe, I began pedaling until I was going faster than I'd ever gone before. The wind was whistling past my ears, and I had to squint my eyes against the force of it. When I neared the bottom turn, I hit my brakes. Now, on a bicycle, your "brakes" simply involve jamming the pedals backward, stopping the chain and slowing the rear tire. But when I jammed the pedals hard, the chain broke.

There was a brief moment when I realized that this was not going to end well, but as I hurtled toward that horseshoe bend, I was able to make a quick decision. I decided to ride into the ditch to my right and lay the bike down to the left, sliding on my side. With any luck, I wouldn't flip over. The plan worked, and I survived. When I came to a stop, I stood up and began walking my bike home. A few minutes later, the pain hit. As I limped gingerly down Hill Street toward home, tears poured from my eyes. I stopped to assess the damage, and noticed that my entire left leg, from ankle to hip, looked like raw hamburger. The injuries didn't concern me as much as the reaction I feared from mom. Typical thinking for a young boy. I was afraid that she wouldn't let me ride my bike to Freck's anymore.

When I got home, she took it rather well. I told her about the chain breaking, and she accepted that explanation. She never asked how fast I'd been going, and I certainly didn't volunteer that information. She cleaned my wounds with soap and water, then applied the red devil liquid known as Mercurochrome. I'm quite certain that it stung more than my injuries. She sent me to my room and I fell asleep. Later that night, I was awakened by a hand on my shoulder. It was Doctor Thrasher, our family physician. Mom had called him to make certain she had treated my wounds correctly, and he told her he would stop by later to check on me.

I hope none of you are confused by that last paragraph. Yes, back in the 1960s, doctors made house calls. They ran regular office hours, then tended to their other patients in the evening. Sometimes, they'd charge a fee, sometimes not. It depended on the patient and the family's financial situation. Drink that in.

As Doc Thrasher examined me, he asked, "How fast do you think you were going when you crashed?" I replied, "It had to be thirty miles an hour, Doc." He nodded and said, "I'd put it closer to forty. You're lucky to be alive son. I'm going to leave the wounds open. They'll heal faster that way. When you begin to get scabs, you can get out and about. Until then, stay inside and mind your mother."

I'd love to tell you that the copperhead snake incident and the bike wreck were my only near death experiences during my four years in Friendly. But they both paled in comparison to what was about to come.

The Day I Almost Died

"Wait, is that a hearse?"

There was a small grass lot beside the Friendly post office where the boys in town would sometimes gather to play baseball during the summer. It was directly across the highway from the elementary school. On the day I almost died, there was a small group of us playing a game there. Mark and Steve Stanley, Jimmy Flescher, Ronnie Williams, Jim and Tom Stewart, and my brother and I.

We split into teams of four. The game was going well until someone on the other team hit a ball across the highway. For some reason, I decided that they weren't going to get a home run so easily, and I sprinted across the highway in pursuit of the ball. What I failed to do was correctly judge the speed of the northbound utility truck. The speed limit was 45 m.p.h., so I felt I had time to cross successfully.

I only remember the sound of tires squealing, and a flash of white light. Then things went dark. When I awoke, I was sitting on the pavement, and the driver of the truck was cradling me in his arms. It took a few moments for my head to clear, and at about the same instant that I began to comprehend that I had been struck by a vehicle, the pain hit. My right leg was bent back under me at an angle that was not normal, and the skin had been ripped from parts of my legs and arms. I knew right away that my leg was broken, but the real pain was from my open wounds (A doctor at the hospital later referred to it as "road rash").

The other boys stood across the road with stunned looks on their ashen faces (I'd later learn that those stunned looks were due to the fact that they couldn't believe I was still alive!). Apparently, my brother had taken off at a dead sprint toward our house to get mom just seconds after the accident occurred. As I sat there crying and being consoled by the driver, I heard a siren in the distance. But before the ambulance could arrive, I saw my mom running toward me at a pace that defied logic. She was actually running faster than my brother, who trailed behind her.

I was so relieved and happy to see her. She wrapped her arms around me and held me so tightly that I forgot my pain for a moment. She asked if I was okay, and I sobbingly informed her that my leg was broken and I hurt all over. After she was sure that I was going to survive, she kicked into mom mode and said, "How many times have I told you to look both ways before you cross the road?" I was shocked. Here I am, hurting and injured, and she's giving me a lecture? But in the back of my mind, I knew she was relieved that I was okay, and that the lecture came from the frustration every parent must experience when their kids don't listen.

By this time, I was feeling a little woozy, and I may have blacked out again. But the sound of the siren getting closer brought me out of my haze, and I looked toward the approaching ambulance. Now, there are times in our lives when we're not sure if we are dreaming, or if what we're seeing is real. You know what I'm talking about if you've ever broken a fever. Sometimes, delirium can play tricks on our minds. As I looked toward the approaching ambulance, I thought, "Wait, is that a hearse?" For a fleeting, terrifying moment, I thought that maybe I had actually been killed.

Unknown to me, the local funeral director in Sistersville also served as the local ambulance driver. This was common in small towns throughout the state back then. Still, seeing a hearse speeding toward me did little to ease my fear. It was only after John Eckels stepped out of the "ambulance" and began administering first aid to me that my mind relaxed. He knew exactly what to do, and he did so with a calm and soothing voice. He told me everything he was doing and why. When it came time to straighten my broken leg, he said, "Son, I'm not going to lie to you. This is going to hurt, but only for a few seconds. I'm going to put an air splint on your leg as soon as I can, and the pain will ease up."

I screamed as soon as he pulled my leg out to straighten it. But true to his word, once he began to inflate the air splint, the throbbing pain went away. I always admired John, because he was the first man to ever talk to me like I was an adult. He did a lot for the communities of Friendly and Sistersville over the years, and I consider him one of my first male role models. But my long journey to healing had just begun, and when we arrived at Sistersville General Hospital, the diagnosis called for surgery in Wheeling, and a long recovery period. I was about to find out how lonely life could be without your family.

The Wheeling Feeling

My Ten Weeks of Recovery

I was transported to the Wheeling Medical Center the same day I was hit by the truck and was immediately sent to surgery. Mom was by my side the entire way, so I felt no fear. I recall the anesthetist telling me to count backward from ten. I made it to seven. When I woke up, there was a steel pin inserted into my knee, and it was attached to a pulley system of weights. They were going to use traction to pull my broken femur back into place, with the hope that it would realign and mend over time.

I was bedridden and placed in the children's ward. I had to lay in that bed, a captive to the pin running through my knee, for nearly three months. Wheeling was forty miles from Friendly, yet my mom somehow managed to visit me nearly every day. I mention this because without the support of her friends and our neighbors, she never could have pulled it off. She had my brother Mark, and my younger sisters Sara and Melissa, to take care of. People in the community stepped up and babysat so mom could visit me. Meals were delivered to our home. It was Friendly people being friendly.

Being a ten-year-old boy in a strange place and being unable to move was frustrating. I made friends, but since I was a long-term resident of the ward, I saw many of them come and go. My only constant was the night charge nurse, Mrs. Black. She was strict when it came to lights out, but on the rare occasions when there were only two or three other kids in the ward, she pretended not to hear our giggling and whispers when she walked by.

The one thing that gave me a sense of power during those months was when the nurse would come in each morning with a menu. I could select whatever I wanted for lunch and dinner, including dessert. Granted, the options were few, and the food was not very good, but being able to choose my meals was pretty cool. Plus, I had ice cream every night for dessert!

I learned about patience during my stay there. Being unable to stand or walk was difficult for a boy my age. Of course, I had no other option, but being able to accept that fact and be okay with it said a lot about my upbringing. Eventually they removed the pin from my leg and placed me in a half-body cast. I was still unable to stand, but the good news was that I could spend the next three weeks recovering at home.

Mom had placed my bed in the room downstairs where she usually did her ironing, just off from the living room. When the ambulance brought me home, the entire family and some neighbors were there to greet me. I was so thrilled to be home, and I was especially looking forward to seeing my baby sister Melissa. She was only two, but I had grown fond of her, and I missed her. As they unloaded me from the ambulance, Melissa took one look at me in my body cast and began crying. She ran into the house, and for the next three months, she seldom visited me. I think she was traumatized by seeing me in that body cast. It broke my heart to see her react that way, because I had been looking forward to seeing her.

There was a steady procession of visitors over those three weeks, and I began to believe that maybe I would be able to bounce back from the reckless act I had committed so many months before. All I wanted to do was run freely again. But when it was time to take the cast off, my doctor warned me that my right leg would be slightly shorter than my left, and I might not be able to run as fast as I used to. That prognosis set me back mentally. When the cast was finally cut off, and I was finally free to walk again, I couldn't.

I went through a week of physical therapy in Wheeling, and they taught me how to walk with crutches. Now home and in my old bedroom, I had a mental block. I used the crutches longer than I should have. I was convinced that I would never be able to put pressure on my right leg again. I was scared to even try.

One morning I woke up and reached for my crutches, which I kept beside my bed. But they weren't there. I saw a note on my nightstand, which read, "Dear Steven. Your crutches are on the other side of your room. If you want them, you can either crawl to them like a baby, or stand up and walk."

I took that first hesitant step, placing weight on my right leg for the first time in five months. I've not stopped walking on it since. A mom knows. Tough love is still love.

The Summer Of '69

My First Job

Dad had determined that mowing our three acres and weeding around the house were now chores my brother and I were old enough to take on. For this, he would pay the princely sum of fifty cents a week in allowance to my brother, while I would receive twenty-five cents. When I protested, dad told me that since my brother was older, he should make more money. I didn't understand what difference age made, especially since we were both doing the same amount of work. But a quarter could buy a bag of chips and a can of soda, two items I seldom had the chance to enjoy. So I kept my silence.

Dad had plowed a corner of the backyard for a small garden that spring, and before he planted seeds, he handed my brother and me a five-gallon bucket each. We were given instructions to fill the buckets with rocks from the tilled soil and empty them into the driveway. All day long, we carried rocks and dumped them, until finally he told us we could quit. He later bragged to the neighbor about how much money he had saved by not having to pay to have fresh gravel brought in for the driveway.

He always found ways to make us earn that allowance. Once the garden began coming in, we would have to water it and pull weeds. This was in addition to our mowing chores. And of course, when mom was cooking, she would dispatch us to the garden to fetch fresh tomatoes, squash, green peppers, etc. Come to think of it, other than plowing the soil and dropping in the seeds, I don't think my dad ever did any work in that garden.

Every Friday that summer, when dad came home from work, he would hand me a quarter, and I would race down to the gas station to buy some Doritos and a can of root beer. Then I would go to my room and slowly enjoy my treats while reading one of my books. That summer, I was reading Tom Sawyer. It was my quiet time, and savoring the words in the book along with my treasured snacks became a tradition. In fact, I soon began associating food with reading, and would often fix a peanut butter and jelly sandwich at lunchtime while reading from my current favorite book.

In July of 1969, mom called me into the dining room and told me to watch the small black-and-white television which sat on the ledge near the window. She said it was important. So I sat there and watched as men talked about space and the moon. I was bored, but mom was totally enthralled, so I kept watching. Suddenly, mom stopped ironing and said, "Listen! They're landing on the moon!" She let out a little yelp of happiness when a crackling voice said, "Houston, the Eagle has landed." I understood that man had just landed on the moon, and that was pretty cool, but I really just wanted to go play. Years later, I understood why mom had called me in to watch that historic moment. She wanted me to be a part of it, even if I didn't appreciate it at the time.

So July turned to August, and I had been saving my allowance for a special treat. There was a small drive-up restaurant on the south end of town called Knowltons Tasty Freeze. It was the only eatery in town, and it was well known for its chili dogs. The owner had a recipe for chili that was unique, and people would drive from up to forty miles away just to buy her hot dogs. But the treat I had my eye on was a root beer float to wash down one of her famous chili dogs. I walked over one afternoon and ordered my treat. I sat at a small table on the side of the building, relishing each bite and sip. After I had finished, I stood up to leave and threw my empty cup and hot dog wrapper into the trash can. I noticed a few pieces of trash on the ground near the trash can, so I picked them up and discarded them without a thought.

As I began to walk home, a voice called out to me. It was Mrs. Knowlton. She had witnessed me picking up the trash, and had come outside. "You're the Winters boy, aren't you?"

"Yes Ma'am."

"Would you like a job?"

"I guess so."

"I need someone to pick up the trash in my parking lot. If you come here twice a day, every day, I'll hire you. All you need to do is pick up trash after the lunch and dinner rush, so I'll need you here at 2:00 p.m. and again at 7:00 p.m. Are you interested?"

"Yes Ma'am."

"Good. I'll call your mom to make sure it's okay. I'll pay you $3.00 a week."

I was quite certain that I had heard her wrong. I was working for a quarter a week, and she was offering how much? I ran home to tell my mom. Mrs. Knowlton had already phoned her, and mom had given permission for my employment. The absolute euphoria that ran through my mind was almost too much to handle. I was going to be rich! But as my joy began to wane later that day, a different kind of happiness emerged. I was waiting for my dad when he pulled into the driveway that evening. I couldn't wait to tell him that I was about to quit his twenty-five-cent a week job.

"Hey dad. I got a new job today!"

He looked at me with his usual disinterest and replied, "Oh really?"

"Yeah, really. And it pays $3.00 a week!"

He arched an eyebrow and walked past me into the house. I heard him arguing with mom a few minutes later. He told her that just because I had a new job, it didn't excuse me from doing the yard work. Mom stood up for me, and she won. Mark was then left to do all the yard and garden chores himself. For this, dad gave him a pay raise of fifty cents a week. Mark was ecstatic. He was now pulling in $1.00 a week in allowance. I never told Mark how much I was making for doing far less work. Sometimes winning is reward enough.

So twice a day I would walk over to Knowltons Tasty Freeze, grab an empty box from the back room, and pick up every single piece of trash in the parking lot. I'd love to tell you that I saved every penny I earned from that job, but in truth, I did not. Every Sunday, when Mrs.

Knowlton placed those three crisp one-dollar bills in my hand, I would walk right around to the order window and spend most of it. I always brought along my favorite book on payday. Getting lost in words while enjoying great food was priceless, and I never regretted spending my wages there. It was my money. My moment. My quiet time.

Wanderlust

Running Errands

I enjoyed running errands for my mom. Any change to the routine of daily life was always fun. Yet I could never simply walk from point A to point B without dallying a bit. I'd often veer off course, distracted by anything of interest which caught my eye. The only times I managed to walk a straight path was when mom sent me to one of the neighbors' houses to borrow something.

The word "borrow" always made me laugh. How do you "borrow" a cup of sugar? You're not going to bring it back. Yet my instructions were clear, and I was given a cup and walked dutifully to whatever house she sent me to. The items mom borrowed were typically eggs, flour, milk, or sugar. So I'd walk up to the neighbor's door and knock, and like a little beggar, I'd politely ask for the item. On rare occasions, the neighbor might request an item from my mom in return. "Yes, I have a cup of sugar she can borrow, but when you get home, ask her if she has any baking soda. A tablespoon will be enough." So I would take the cup of sugar home, give mom the neighbor's request, then walk back with the baking soda.

This bartering system was common in Friendly. Just before suppertime on any given night, you might see children marching from house to house carrying measuring cups like a small army of begging vagrants. Most moms still cooked and baked meals from scratch, so this network of cooperation between neighbors was vital to prevent trips to the only grocery store in town. Besides, on Wednesdays, the egg and milk man would come through and restock everyone. But more on him later.

As I stated earlier, when sent out on other errands, I tended to take the scenic route, so to speak. Mom was a smoker, and she preferred a particular brand of cigarettes called "Eve." This is a part of history which might bewilder some of you, but back in the day, mom would give me money to buy her a pack of cigarettes, and the merchants would sell said cigarettes to me. It was common for moms to send their kids out to buy tobacco products, whether it be smokes for them or chewing tobacco and snuff for the dads. The moms would call the store and let them know what their kids would be buying, and since the merchants knew us, they didn't bat an eye.

Mom usually combined the cigarette errand with her only other vice, Pepsi-Cola. I was given a cardboard carton holding eight empty sixteen-ounce glass bottles, which I took to the store. There was a five-cent deposit on each bottle, so they had to be returned for an exchange when you purchased a new carton of Pepsi. The old bottles were placed in front of the grocery store, where they would be picked up by the Pepsi delivery man on his next visit. Mom always called the store to let them know I was coming. Usually, I took my time getting there. I might spy some tadpoles in a creek, or see one of my friends playing in the school lot. It didn't take much to distract me.

If too much time had passed, and I had not yet returned home, mom kicked in her personal GPS system. Of course, the actual GPS system we use today wasn't available to common folk at that time, but trust me, hers was just as effective. She would call the store and ask if I had left yet. "Yes, he left about twenty minutes ago. I think he was walking toward the post office." Then, a few more calls, placed to strategic location centers (i.e., other moms) along the path I should be taking home. They would in turn call other moms, and within a matter of minutes, my exact location had been pinpointed and reported. My meandering usually ended with a mom walking out onto her porch as I passed by and saying, "Your mother wants you home now!" Small town moms back then were always on the lookout for other kids. They were the original GPS.

Okay, getting back to the milk and egg man. Most families only had one car, and when the dads were at work, the moms were basically stuck at home. So how did they get their basic groceries? Enter home delivery, circa the 1960s. There was a metal insulated box which sat on most people's doorsteps or porches. Once a week, a delivery man would come to your home and bring milk, eggs, and butter. The system was simple. He would leave a blank order form inside a small envelope attached to the side of the box. You would check off the items you wanted him to deliver the following week, then place your payment in the envelope along with the order form. When he made the deliveries, he would take your order form and payment, then leave another blank one. He soon expanded his offerings to include ice cream and popsicles, which were always a special treat to those who could afford such things.

This system attracted other entrepreneurs. Local bakeries began offering home delivery of bread, doughnuts, and pastries of all sorts. Diaper-cleaning services were also quite popular, as there was no such thing as "disposable" diapers back in the day. Diapers were made of cloth, and when soiled, they needed to be cleaned for reuse. When moms saw this opportunity to reduce their laundry load, they jumped at it. It was a profitable business, although I doubt the employee who had to drive around all day picking up dirty diapers was thrilled with his career choice.

The Gunslinger

Whippings

Many of us have heard the phrase, "Wait until your father gets home," while growing up. It was a threat issued by every mom back in the day, and we all knew exactly what it meant, didn't we? (I can see your head nodding up and down) It was mom throwing down the gauntlet and sending us to our rooms to await the punishment that only dad seemed capable of doling out. It was the dreaded whipping.

Allow me to lay this out in simple terms. If a kid did something bad that merited punishment, they were subject to a whipping. Moms back in the day didn't use "time outs." The purpose of a whipping was to make kids understand that there were actual consequences to their bad behavior. A "time out" for a misbehaving child is akin to a cop without a gun yelling at a fleeing felon, "Halt, or I'll yell halt again!" It just doesn't work. There must be consequences, even if they are painful. I never liked getting a whipping, but when I did, you can bet that that bad behavior was never repeated again.

When it came down to the severity of the crime, mom was the judge and the jury. If the crime was a minor one, she would carry out the sentence herself. This required us to go outside, select a switch from her lilac bush, and bring it to her. If the switch met her approval, she would give us several hard swats on the butt. If we brought back a switch that was too small, she would select one herself, and we would receive twice the number of swats.

But for the more serious offenses, she would send us to our rooms to wait for dad to get home. Now, I didn't get sent to my room a lot, but when I did, there was a very real sense of dread. All I could do all day long was to wait for the sound of my dad's car tires crunching the gravel in the driveway, knowing that pain was soon to follow. This was, of course, a very effective part of the punishment. It was like being on death row. You never knew exactly when the executioner would come, but you knew it would be soon.

Dad was never in a good mood when he came home from work. He was tired and hungry, and he just wanted to unwind peacefully after supper and watch the news. When met by my mom with news of my transgression, he would stomp up the steps and come down the hall toward my room. The fear I felt was intense, because I was sure that in another life, my dad was a gunslinger.

When he appeared at my bedroom door, he would stare at me, not saying a word. I would sit on the edge of my bed and began to cry, knowing what was coming. His eyes were cold, and his gaze was unflinching (Picture Clint Eastwood or Matt Dillon in their heydays). With a single flick of his wrist, he would unhook his belt, then pull it out of the loops so fast I would only hear a "whoosh." If he had been facing an outlaw in the Old West, dad would surely have outdrawn him.

Without being told, I would roll over onto my stomach and wait. Dad would rain down several hard licks to my butt, but he always seemed to lighten up on the last two. He left without ever saying a word. I never knew why he always eased up. I only received a few whippings from him as I grew up. Maybe he knew that I wasn't a bad kid. But it was thanks to my big brother's bright idea (and my stupidity for believing it) that I received the most brutal, and last, whipping from dad.

It was a cold December day. Mark and I had been arguing in his room, and, as usual, it had escalated into fisticuffs. At some point, an antique lamp was broken. Mom pronounced sentence immediately, and we were confined to quarters. While awaiting dad's arrival home, Mark came up with an idea. To avoid the severity of dad's blows, he would stuff comic books down his pants. My first thought was, "This will never work," but my next thought was, "Why not?" When dad arrived home and came upstairs to dole out our punishment, we both assumed the position on the bed. His first strike landed on the back of my leg, and I let out a scream. He had missed the comic books completely. Then he struck Mark fully on the butt....and there was a weird "'thock" sound as the comic books absorbed the blow. Enraged, dad made us take off our pants, and he began to rain down blow after blow with his belt on our naked backsides.

When mom came to our room later for the obligatory "I hope you learned your lesson" speech, she saw the welts on our bare legs. She began to cry, and she hugged us both before leaving the room without saying a word. A few minutes later, we heard her yelling at dad downstairs. From that day on, we never received another whipping from dad.

The Night Stalker

My Brother's Talent

❖

As much as I joke about my older brother in this book, I do love him. But back in the day? Not so much! Besides the fact that he was bigger and stronger, and that he used to pick on me, he was also selfish, and he had an appetite that never seemed to be satisfied. This combination of selfishness and hunger made him a legendary predator at night. You've already read about his behavior at mom's card parties, but that's just the tip of the iceberg.

My brother's main weakness was knowing there was food in the house, which was meant for everyone. To him, having first dibs was vital. This was most prevalent on Friday evenings, when mom made her grocery store trip. She would put away the groceries, which would sometimes include some "goodies," and Mark would watch, like a criminal casing his next heist, making notes on which items he intended to plunder during the night. Then he would put his plan into action.

His favorite ploy was asking mom if he could sleep on the couch on Friday nights, claiming his room was either too hot or too cold, depending on the season. Mom would give her approval, and he would lay there quietly, waiting for the household to fall asleep. Like a master thief, he would steal into the kitchen and feast upon the goodies intended for all of us, reveling in the fact that he was the first to taste them.

One of his most memorable thefts occurred when mom had relented to my constant pleas for Lucky Charms cereal. She didn't think it was worth the money, but I had begged her, and so she finally bought a box. When I went to bed that night, all I could think about was sitting down in front of the television with my bowl of Lucky Charms and watching my favorite cartoons.

When I awoke on Saturday morning and passed by Mark's room, I noticed that he was in his bed. I didn't give it much thought, even though he had asked mom if he could sleep on the couch the night before. I figured he had gotten scared or too cold and had come up to his room during the night. I ran down the steps and into the kitchen, grabbing a bowl from the cupboard and a spoon from the drawer. I then opened the fridge, pulled out the milk, and eagerly reached into the pantry for the cereal I had been dreaming about.

The first thing I noticed was that the cereal box had been opened. I didn't give that much thought, because mom and dad always went to bed after us kids, so they might have had a bowl. After all, it wasn't the usual type of cereal we kept in the house, so maybe they had tried it. But as I poured the cereal into my bowl, there was something missing, something very important—there were no marshmallows. Not a single one. I grabbed a larger bowl from the cupboard and emptied the entire cereal box into it. No marshmallows. It was at that moment that I realized what had happened. The night stalker had struck. Having gorged himself on the marshmallows, Mark had returned to his room.

There were other instances of his thievery. When mom would buy Neapolitan ice cream, he would scoop out the chocolate and strawberry, leaving the vanilla. When mom would leave a partially empty Pepsi-Cola in the fridge, she would often find it empty in the morning.

Once mom figured out who was doing this, she became more clever at hiding the goodies. But the night stalker was too sly and smart. Mom would hide ice cream bars behind the meat in the freezer, but they would disappear. She would hide candy in empty margarine bowls in the fridge, but they, too, would disappear. If there was a goodie in the house, the night stalker could sniff it out. He was relentless. He was the best.

Pure Imagination

Entertainment

◈

We only had three television channels to choose from, and what we watched was solely dependent on whatever our parents wanted to watch. Only on Saturday mornings did we have free reign to watch cartoons. The Flintstones, Bugs Bunny, and The Jetsons were just a few of our favorites. I do recall one show that disturbed me though. It was called H.R. Puffinstuff. To this day I have no idea what that thing was supposed to be. He was our version of Barney, but at least kids of later generations knew that Barney was a purple dinosaur.

The rest of the week, our television viewing was basically at the will of our parents. Dad would usually place one of us near the front of the television when watching the news after supper. He did this because there was no remote control. You had to change the channels manually by turning the knob on the front of the television to the corresponding number. Each time one station would go to commercial, dad would shout out the number he wanted us to turn to. This was how parents used to "surf channels" back in the day.

Thankfully, there were a few shows my parents liked that I liked as well, and one of them was Star Trek. The show was far ahead of its time, although it didn't garner much in the way of ratings back then. But it made a lasting impression on me (In fact, I still watch reruns to this day). I would incorporate Star Trek into my imagination whenever there was an approaching thunderstorm. Once the wind picked up and the sky darkened, I would rush into the house and run upstairs. There was a window at the end of the hallway which faced west toward the river. Dad had placed an antique school desk there as decor—but for me, it was the captain's chair on the U.S.S. Enterprise!

I would imagine that I was Captain Kirk, and that my ship was entering an ion storm. Then I would go into full pretend mode.

"Shields up, Mr. Sulu!"

"Steady!"

"Lieutenant Uhura, sound Red Alert!"

"All hands, this is the captain. Brace yourself."

"Scotty, how are the shields holding up?"

"Spock, any readings on the intensity of the storm?"

I would sit there until the storm had passed, thrilled by the rush I experienced using pure imagination. I suppose you too, dear reader, likely had a special imaginary place you visited when you were young. I encourage you to remember it now.

Despite the impact of Star Trek on my youth, it was reading, not television, that truly opened up my imagination. I began to see things not as they were, but in a "what if" way. I remember thinking when mom bought me a bag of tiny green molded-plastic army men figures, "What if they're real? Can they hear me? Maybe they just can't move."

I realized at a young age that just because we're told "what" something is, that doesn't mean it couldn't be something else entirely. When I would wander through the woods, or play near the creek, I was fascinated by what I saw. There was a whole world of living creatures all around me, yet no one paid much attention to them. Caterpillars, frogs, butterflies, lightning bugs, ants, etc.

All serving their own purpose and living quietly among us. Yet humans paid them no mind.

I always looked forward to late June, because that's when the lightning bugs (or fire flies to some) appeared. Just before dusk, I would beg mom for a mason jar, and she would punch holes in the lid so the lightning bugs could breathe after being caught. I would run out to the big field between our house and Route 2 and grab as many of them as I could. I'd place them in the jar, and when I had a few dozen, I'd steal off to my room, shut off the light, and stare at them for hours. Their blinking tails amazed me. How did they do it?

I had the same fascination with tadpoles. There was a small creek that ran along that same big field and underneath Route 2, and in it were numerous pools of stagnant water where frogs would lay their eggs. I would scoop up a handful of eggs, once again using a mason jar, and keep them in my room. Each day they would grow a little, soon forming tails and breaking free of their clear egg sacks. They would slowly morph into tiny frogs, and it was amazing to watch.

Observing these creatures gave me a unique perspective on life at an early age. It seemed to me that if we ignored the amazing things we *know* are there, what else is there that we *refuse to see*? Thus began my journey into the world of imagination. While kids today get lost in the world of video games, I became lost in my own world. Every object, no matter how small or obscure, became a subject of my imagination. A jar found buried in the mud along a hillside became a magical talisman left there generations ago by a wizard. I cannot count the number of adventures I went on back then. But they were all wonderful, and they were all created by me.

Some of my favorite imaginary adventures were spent in the large porcelain bathtub (with the clawed feet) in our upstairs bathroom. Mom had purchased a bottle of a new product called Mr. Bubbles, which was supposed to make bath time fun for kids. It did! The mountains of bubbles were like a playground for me. I used some of the plastic "boats" from Knowltons Tasty Freeze as ships, but mom quickly put a stop to that. Apparently, using discarded trash in a bathtub does not meet parental approval. As a preteen, I saw nothing wrong with it, but I found an alternative.

One of my dad's favorite hobbies was models. He would spend hours gluing together cars and ships. Since mom had forbid me from using the plastic boats from Knowltons, I figured that one or two of his battleship models would replace them quite nicely. After all, they were just sitting on a shelf gathering dust. I had some epic sea battles with those ships! Unfortunately, the ships didn't survive fully intact. This may have led to one of those whippings I deserved.

I haven't spent a minute in a bathtub since those days. We didn't have the option of taking a shower back then, because we didn't have one. And yet, buying a bottle of Mr. Bubbles and sinking into a hot bath again some day is on my bucket list.

My imagination also helped me survive troublesome times. Mom and dad were going through a divorce in 1972, and it was impossible not to hear their fights late at night as I lay in bed. I saw less and less of dad during that year, and while mom never showed it, I knew she was sad and hurting.

Just before the end of summer vacation, my dad pulled into the driveway. Another car pulled in behind him, and a family piled out. It was the Summers family, and I soon found out they were buying our house. It was difficult to comprehend that someone else would be sleeping in my room. I didn't want to leave this house. Who would guide the U.S.S. Enterprise when the storms approached from the western sky?

The following week, we packed up and moved to Sistersville. Mom and dad had divorced. The magical kingdom was gone. But it has survived in my heart.

Still Living Friendly

My Landing Pad

Fifty years later, I still occasionally return to Friendly. My daughter and two grandsons now live in a small house at the top of Friendly Hill. When I leave my home in North Carolina to go visit them, a little part of me gets excited. As I sit in my car and start the engine, I can still hear Captain Kirk's voice in my head: "Steady as she goes. Ahead warp factor one, Mister Sulu." When I finally pull into my daughter's yard eight hours later, I always post on Facebook, "The Eagle has landed."

There are some memories that are so deeply embedded in our minds that we can never forget them. Nor should we try. Knowing that I can return to that magical kingdom is comforting. Although many of the people I knew growing up in Friendly have moved on or passed away, I can still sense them when I'm home. There is an unseen aura which still surrounds this tiny West Virginia village. It's composed of the spirit of hard work and simple pleasures. It's reflected in each new generation, and it's built on the backs of those who came before them.

As the fog began to gently roll into Friendly from the Ohio River on my last trip home, I sat on my daughter's porch and thought about my youth. I gazed up at the stars and realized they were still in the same place above me as they were fifty years ago. I thought about all the people who had touched my life when I was a young boy.

The stars began to fade slowly as the fog grew thicker, and as the mist began to fall gently upon my skin, a tear rolled down my cheek. Those people were still here. Still touching me. Still raising me. Still watching me. Still caring for me.

Fifty years later, I am still growing up.....Friendly.

Acknowledgements

It would be impossible to acknowledge every person who helped develop my life during the four-year period this book covers. I'll name a few, but please forgive me if I exclude you. After all, it has been fifty years!

First and foremost, I want to thank my Mamaw, Thelma Christopher, for always being a constant in my life. I love you more than you'll ever know. You're an amazing woman! (As of the writing of this book, Mamaw celebrated her 98th birthday!).

Thanks to Howard and Mary Mace. You were great neighbors, and you gave me wonderful memories. Thanks to Sue Stewart, Barbara and Ross Shuman, Peggy Mosser, Susan Stoneking, Bob and Esther Davis, Virginia Knowlton, Phil and Nancy Stanley, Mary Bell, Bill and Ramona Williamson, and a host of others.

Obviously, I acknowledge my mom, Barbara Winters. I miss you so much! You were brave, and you instilled courage and ethics in each of your kids. You shielded us from the problems you were going through with dad. You protected us and never complained. You were, are, and always will be my inspiration.

Thanks to my siblings Mark, Sara, and Melissa. I love each of you. Although the years have spread us out across the country, you're all in my heart each day. Mark, I poke fun at you in this book, but know that I always looked up to you, even when you stole my food!. You shared my love and passion for sports, and you were my best friend. Sara, you remind me so much of Mamaw Winters. You're always taking care of others, and you're a fantastic Mamaw. Melissa, you have always held a special place in my heart. I see so much of mom in you, and I know she's proud of you. But I'm still gonna call you Missy.

A special thank you to Abe and Betty Cowgill, who have been so instrumental in raising my grandsons. Melanie and the boys are blessed to have you, and I am thankful for all you have done.

My last thank you is to Linda Sole. She was like my second mom. She encouraged me to write my first book, and without her pushing me, I never would have done it. I will never forget that, and I will never forget her. That's a promise I will always keep. Never forget where you come from...or the people who helped you along the way.

I leave you with a quote from an esteemed educator and storyteller I admire very much, Mr. Joseph Hickman, "Do good works, and care for each other."

Indeed. That's the Friendly way. The Tyler County way. The West Virginia way.

THE END

My Books

(Series)

A Knight in the 'Ville - Why the Babies Cry

A Knight in the 'Ville - The December Dark

A Knight in the 'Ville - Beneath the Bricks

A Knight in the 'Ville - Grave Concerns

A Knight in the 'Ville - The Diary

(Novel)
The Meter Man

(Short Stories)
Ghosts on the Ohio

Printed in the United States
By Bookmasters